Sea Smoke

PROSE POEMS BY

Louis Jenkins

BOOKS BY LOUIS JENKINS

The Winter Road (2000)
Just Above Water (1997)
Nice Fish: New and Selected Prose Poems (1995)
All Tangled Up With the Living (1991)
An Almost Human Gesture (1987)

Sea Smoke

PROSE POEMS BY

Louis Jenkins

HOLY COW! PRESS • DULUTH, MINNESOTA • 2004

Text ©2004 by Louis Jenkins.
Cover painting, "Funding for the Arts,"
oil on canvas (16.5 x 19 inches), by Scott Murphy.
Author photograph by Amy Burkett.

Thanks to the editors of the following publications in which some of these
poems appeared: *Borealis, Great River Review, Jubilat, Key Stach(el), Lake Country
Journal, Luna, Manhattan Reivew, Minneapolis Tribune, Paragraph, Redactions,
Ruby, Sentence, Speakeasy, Tarpaulin Sky, Terminus, The Ninth Letter, The
Thousands, Three Candles, To Topio, Utne, Water-Stone, Willow Springs.*

Library of Congress Cataloging-in-Publication Data

Jenkins, Louis, 1942-
Sea Smoke: poems / by Louis Jenkins.
p. cm.
ISBN 0-930100-13-1 (paper: alk. paper)
1. Middle West—Poetry. 2. Minnesota—Poetry.
3. Nature—Poetry. 4. Family—Poetry.
1. Title.
PS3560.E488S43   2004
811' .54—DC22   2004042397

Holy Cow! Press books are distributed to the trade by Consortium Book Sales
and Distribution, 1045 Westgate Drive, Saint Paul, Minnesota 55114.
For personal orders and inquiries, please write to:

Holy Cow! Press
Post Office Box 3170
Mount Royal Station
Duluth, Minnesota 55803

CONTENTS

I

Imaginary Reader   9
The Body and the Soul   10
Blue Moon   11
The Talk   12
Culinary Considerations   13
The Kiss   14
The First Day of Spring   15
Fisherman   16
A Happy Song   17
The Back Country   18
Heredity   19
Where Go the Boats   20
Canaries   21

II

Canadian Wilderness   25
Overboard   26
The Clouds   27
Bassoon   28
Free Lawn Mower   29
Popples   30
Surveying   31
Wedding   32
Sleeping Beauty   33
July   34
I Saw Mama Kissing Santa Claus   35
A Sense of Direction   36

III

Retirement   39
Autumn Leaves   40
Haldeman & Erlichman   41
Middle Ages   42

Awakening   43
Apple Dolls   44
The Ash Grove   45
Diner   46
Fictional Character   47
Old Couple   48
Hitchhiker   49
Knife Island   50
Steady or Slowly Falling   51
Park   52
Time Marches On   53

IV

Sublimation   57
The Long Winter   58
An Ill Wind   59
I Must Say   60
The Black Journal   61
Dark Days   62
Lost   63
Goings On Around the House   64
Old Friends   65
The State of the Economy   66
Remember   67
Of an Age   68
Some Things to Think About   69
The Chair   70
Wayfaring Stranger   71
The Snowman Monologues   72
Wednesday   73
Expanding Universe   74
Up in the Morning   75
Wrong Turn   76

I

IMAGINARY READER

If poetry is your life, then your life must be the poem, a life that exists only for the reader. And who is the reader for whom you write? The imaginary reader? Perhaps the reader is a beautiful woman, so taken with the words that she reads late into the night, propped on one elbow. Only a sheet covers the curve of her hip, slipping away from her bare shoulder. The summer breeze from the window teases her dark hair. Her lips move from time to time, ever so slightly, as she repeats a phrase. . . . But probably, the imaginary reader is even more vaguely described, like God. The reader reads. Nothing happens. Nothing changes. The night goes on. He is still reading. He yawns, rubs his eyes. Any moment now the book might slip from his hands, so you write faster.

THE BODY AND THE SOUL

Long ago I was told that the body was the temple of the soul, a temporal dwelling for the eternal soul. I suppose the body could be thought of as a dwelling, it has plumbing and electricity. I think in most cases, however, it's more like a modest bungalow than a temple. And the house idea does not accommodate human mobility. Perhaps a motor home would be a better analogy. The body is the motor home of the soul where the soul sits behind the wheel and drives the body here and there, back and forth to work, off to the seashore or the Rocky Mountains. But the soul is a bad driver, so often distracted, dwelling on higher things, pondering, moving slowly up the pass, traffic backed up behind for miles. The soul gazes idly out the windows (eyes) paying no attention whatsoever to the road, and is in danger of sending the entire metaphor plunging over the precipice.

BLUE MOON

The moon looks worried, rising above the Lake. The moon looks so unhappy, so pale. The moon has not been well. The moon has had a lot of problems with meteors, especially in youth. And night after night, the same earth rises . . . . It hasn't been easy for the moon. The moon. . . The moon. . . The moon this, and the moon that. You drive faster, but the moon keeps pace, looking sadly into your car window. "Why are you leaving," the moon wonders, "and where will you go?"

THE TALK

He liked her immediately, her blue eyes, the way she listened, as if what he said was fascinating, the easy, natural way she laughed at all his jokes. Her rather conventional good looks and dress belied her intelligence. They had things in common, an interest in art and humanism. She talked about the problems of coffee growers in Central America. He listened, but he also thought about kissing her on the neck, where her blond hair curled just behind her ear. He thought about other things, too. Mostly they laughed. Then she was silent. She looked at him. He saw that her eyes were gray, not blue. She was serious. She said, "Matt, this has gone too far in too short a time. I feel as though I'm being smothered. I have no time to myself anymore. I feel like you are always there. And I can't even so much as speak to another man. . ." "What are you talking about?" he said, "We only met an hour ago!" "That is exactly what I'm trying to say," she said.

CULINARY CONSIDERATIONS

Lyle can't eat any onions or garlic. Ann can only eat onions if they are well cooked and cut into very tiny pieces. Jim is extremely allergic to nuts. Phil is allergic to shellfish. Steve has a violent reaction to celery. Patricia is allergic to beef. Connie cannot eat processed meat. No fat for Joe. Dennis cannot eat any spicy food. Frank believes he is allergic to vinegar. Georganne is unable to tolerate mayonnaise. Michael is allergic to eggs and certain fish. Charlie and Sue do not eat meat, except fish. Dylan eats no meat or dairy products, except once when he ate an entire large pizza. Peter will not eat cheese. Thomas will eat no vegetables. Richard won't eat anything. Almost no one drinks anymore except Walt, who drinks too much and has to be sent home in a taxi. Elaine cannot stand Joann so they have to be seated at opposite ends of the table.

THE KISS

When I was eleven or twelve years old, I thought a lot about kissing girls. Since I had never kissed a girl, romantically, that is, I was unsure how to go about it. I tried to imagine grabbing a girl roughly, as sometimes happened in movies, turning her around and kissing her hard on the lips. ("She struggled a moment then succumbed to the power of his passionate kiss . . .") Betsy O'Reilly would have knocked me down. How much pressure did one apply, should the lips just touch, lightly? (I had never heard of French kissing.) And what was the duration of a kiss? The movies of that day often ended with a long kiss, the couple embraced, the music rose, but then the image faded. After the kiss what happens? Do you just stand there sort of embarrassed, shuffling your feet? You'd have to say something, but what? "Thank you for the really swell kiss, Alexandra?" The logistics were formidable. I thought about kissing a lot, but I began to see that it was impossible.

THE FIRST DAY OF SPRING

When one is young, every day (as I remember it) is the first day of spring, all headlong and heedless. But, as it turns out, life really is short and before you know it you are old and filled with sadness. Nothing to do now but watch the birds, scratch a few petroglyphs for someone to puzzle over years from now, stay out of the way and leave the bulk of the wanton destruction to those who are younger. The human race will evolve or go extinct. So what? It happens all the time. You never see saber-toothed tigers anymore. I suppose I should be sorry about that, but to tell the truth, I never liked them. All that screaming and prowling around outside the house at night—who needs it?

FISHERMAN

Here's an old guy talking to himself. He reels in his bait and says, "Son, you've got to go out there again. I know the rocks are treacherous, the water is deep. The winds can come up suddenly, and there's no more than the thinnest line ties you to me. This is the way your life is going to be, out and back, again and again, partly in this world, partly in the other, never at home in either. Still, it's what you were born to do. You are young and strong, all steel and hooks. You know I'll do everything I can to bring you back safely. Go out there boy, and bring home a big fish for your old father to eat."

A HAPPY SONG

We know that birds' singing has to do with territory and breeding rights. Male birds sing to attract females and warn away other males. These songs include threat and intimidation, and perhaps, in the more complicated songs, the insinuation of legal action. It's the grim business of earning a living in a grim world. Each song has its own subtle sound, the idiosyncrasies of its singer. It turns out, though, that the females don't really value innovation and invention and generally mate with males that sing the most ordinary, traditional tune. There is always, though, some poor sap that doesn't get it, sitting alone on his branch practicing and polishing his peculiar version until it flows smoothly as water through the streambed, a happy song that fills us with joy on this first warm day of the year.

THE BACK COUNTRY

When you are in town, wearing some kind of uniform is helpful, policeman, priest, etcetera. Driving a tank is very impressive, or a car with official lettering on the side. If that isn't to your taste, you could join the revolution, wear an armband, carry a homemade flag tied to a broom handle, or a placard bearing an incendiary slogan. At the very least, you should wear a suit and carry a briefcase and a cell phone, or wear a team jacket and a baseball cap and carry a cell phone. If you go into the woods, the back country, someplace past all human habitation, it is a good idea to wear orange and carry a gun, or, depending on the season, carry a fishing pole, or a camera with a big lens. Otherwise, it might appear that you have no idea what you are doing, that you are merely wandering the earth, no particular reason for being here, no particular place to go.

HEREDITY

I have come to recognize certain genetic traits that have been handed down to me, patterns of behavior, certain involuntary actions. I can feel them happening, that worried look of my mother's, that almost angry, I-deserve-better-than-this look. And my father's cough, the sleeves of his work shirt rolled to the elbow, a pencil poised motionless above a scrap of paper lying on the yellow oilcloth that covers the table, next to the white porcelain salt and pepper shakers with the red metal tops. Which means it must be sometime in the 1940s, the war still going on. Neither of them saying a word, as if stunned there in the dim late night light of the kitchen. And what am I doing here? I should have been in bed hours ago.

WHERE GO THE BOATS

Green leaves a-floating
Castles of the foam,
Boats of mine a-boating—
Where will all come home?

R. L. Stevenson

Legend has it that the great Chinese poet Li Po made his newly composed poems into paper boats and let them float away down the Yangtze. I recommend this practice to poets of today, particularly beginning poets, as an alternative to submitting poems to literary magazines. I do this chiefly because I believe that the chances of your poem actually being read are greater using this method.

Suppose, by some mischance, some failure of the system, your poem is published. It won't be read. Just the words "literary magazine" are enough to send a chill to the heart of the most voracious reader.

How much more noble to think of your poem plying the waters of the Susquehanna or the Verdigris or the Mississippi. Think of your poem being pulled ashore by an astonished reader in Davenport or Baton Rouge. Or imagine your little poem boat sailing at last into the open sea, bravely alone.

CANARIES

I remember when I was a child, I had a pair of canaries in a cage in my bedroom. I had the idea that I would raise and sell canaries. I asked one of my sisters if she remembered them. She remembered that they were parakeets, not canaries. I asked another sister. She said she didn't remember any canaries, but she remembered how mean I was to her. My youngest sister doesn't remember having birds, but thinks that we had a pet rabbit. I don't remember that. My brother thinks we had a pet crow that talked. I don't remember a crow but I remember we had a myna bird for a while that said, "How ya doin'?", but he belonged to someone else. My mother says that she would never have allowed birds in the house. I remember how the female canary ignored the male, but chirped plaintively to a mockingbird that sang outside my window all summer long.

II

THE CANADIAN WILDERNESS

I was awakened during the night by something inside my sleeping bag rubbing against my back near my shoulder blade, scratching me. I reached around and it felt like one of those stiff cloth labels, the kind they attach to pillows and mattresses and such, the ones that say DO NOT REMOVE UNDER PENALTY OF LAW. I grabbed hold and gave it a yank, and much to my shock, found that it was attached to my back! I lay there a few moments, my mind racing, my back still in pain where I'd pulled at the label. I tried to calm down. I must have been dreaming. I felt again, carefully. It was definitely attached to my back. I didn't know what to do. Should I wake the others, say, "I've got a mattress label attached to my back!" What could they do, anyway? It isn't really a medical emergency and we're camped deep in the Canadian wilderness, no phones, no roads, a hundred miles from the nearest settlement. Outside the sky is clear, a nearly full moon shining over the lake, no sound except for a little breeze in the spruce trees. It's beautiful. Nowhere to go, nothing to be done.

OVERBOARD

A piece of folded paper comes flying down from the deck above, over the stern of the excursion boat, and I have the split-second shock of something irretrievably lost. Well, it isn't a child overboard. It isn't even the Magna Charta, pitched into the deep. Perhaps it's an old love letter, written in a loopy hand with little hearts dotting the i's, thrown ceremoniously by someone at the end of a marriage or an affair. Maybe it's the plans for a failed invention, or the first page of a bad novel. Most likely, there's just some dope up above pitching garbage, a shopping list, or nothing, a blank piece of paper. It is just something that happened, anything, made memorable only by circumstance. The paper lingers there in the flat water at the center of the boat's wake and then, before you know it, is ten years past, a tiny speck. And then it's gone.

THE CLOUDS

The clouds sweep toward the western horizon as if they were nomads. Horses, men, children, dogs and wives, cook pots and knives, feathers, flags, ribbons, and hides, skulls borne on tall poles, all caught up in the whirl, the ecstasy of motion. They set off with a will, as if inspired. It is as if they served the great Kahn himself, a man of such presence that simply to behold his majesty removes any doubt. To hear him speak banishes all hesitation. Onward! They would follow him across continents, across oceans if necessary.... But the thoughtless clouds move only at the behest of the wind. Who is no one at all.

BASSOON

The very slightest of winds moves the curtains, the violins faint tremolo just before dawn. Then you hear again the voice you know so well, a voice at once your own and not your own, a voice that may have gone on all night long and, for all you know, may continue long after your eyes have closed. The sound of a bassoon, perhaps, that wanders vaguely as a bumblebee from flower to brick wall to water bucket, yet is clear and sweet in the early light before the full cacophony of the day begins. Birdsong. Children's voices. Flutes and piccolos, quick, high-pitched and somewhat annoying. "Oh, Grandpa," they say, "not another one of your long, boring stories!"

FREE LAWN MOWER

There's a broken down lawn mower at the curbside with a sign saying, "FREE." And so I ask myself, what does freedom mean to a lawn mower? A lawn mower that has only one job and no outside interests, a job which it can no longer perform? Gone the days of the engine's roar, the cloud of blue smoke, the open lawn, the waves of cut grass left in its wake, the flying gravel, the mutilated paper cup. Freedom could only mean the freedom to rust away into powder and scale. Most likely the lawn mower will be thrown into the back of a beat-up truck by a guy who sees its potential as scrap, a guy who will seize upon anything of even the slightest value, anything free.

POPPLES

In places where there are fewer trees, people call them aspen and they are highly prized. Up here they are known as popples, scrap wood. Not very good for lumber or firewood, but good enough for paper, and the armyworms love them. They grow everywhere. Wherever there's an opening, the popples move in, any abandoned clearing, any yard left untended. Popples are excitable, quivering all over at the slightest hint of a breeze, full of stupid chatter, gossip, rumor and innuendo. The proletarian popple tree, growing, optimistic, got the kids all working, grandkids on the way. . .

Popples are lovely in fall when the leaves turn yellow and gold, or in winter with a new moon caught in the branches, and in spring when the rain enhances the delicate grey-green color of the bark. I wouldn't mind a view like this when I come to the bottom of the slide into old age and senility: a stand of popples judiciously framed by the bedroom window to exclude the junk car and the trash cans just to the right.

SURVEYING

One of the first jobs I had was surveyor's helper. There were three or four of us in a crew; we worked all over Oklahoma and west Texas, surveying lines for power lines or gas pipelines. In brushy country this could be a slow process, since trees and other obstacles had to be cleared from the line of sight. The best surveying was in the high plains of west Texas. Here the transit man could see for miles. Two of us walked, measured the distance and drove stakes. The last member of the party was the engineer, the boss, who wrote down figures in a little book. Most of what we'd do would be to mark a straight line across the country, from point A to point B, making calculated turns only when absolutely necessary. All very precise, in theory. It was a good job. We got to travel, eat in greasy cafes and sleep in dumpy motels. In the evening we drank beer and teased the girls in the bar. Best of all I was young and free. Here were the endless plains, the vast cloudless sky. I could walk across Texas forever. As long as it was in a straight line.

THE WEDDING

"Where is the wedding? What time does it start?" "I don't know. What did you do with the invitation? What shall I wear?" Someone said it was at St. Paul's then someone else said that at the last minute the couple decided to fly to Las Vegas and get married at a drive-up chapel. Never mind. It's the ideal wedding. The ideal couple.

Turns out we've missed the ceremony. As we arrive the minister is walking away from the church carrying his robes over his arm. It was hotter than usual today. He is smiling slightly as he walks, thinking of the newlyweds, thinking of a gin and tonic.

The old folks have gathered on the church lawn to chat. Summer hats, white shoes, pink dresses, powder blue sport coats. "Who was the bride?" No one is sure. The granddaughter of a friend? A distant cousin's niece? "But wasn't the bride beautiful?" "And the groom, so handsome—well, everyone says he's smart, has a very important job."

Meanwhile the bride and groom have gone to the rose garden to be photographed. Clouds are gathering in the west. Thunderstorms are predicted. It makes us unreasonably happy to see the bride and groom in their silly outfits, smiling at the camera—the air full of threat and promise, the smell of rain and of roses.

SLEEPING BEAUTY

Everything outside had changed, the faces, the styles, the landscape was altered, even the language had changed, making it difficult for the people to understand the nobility. At first the outsiders had been curious and those inside the castle had a kind of celebrity status. But the novelty wore off. In the new world there was no need for these ancients. The prince and his crew ran everything and though the prince loved the princess, there was no getting around it, the age difference was a factor in their relationship, she being exactly 100 years older than the prince. At times she found his immaturity trying. He spent so much time away from the castle in the company of knights he brought from his father's kingdom, involved in politics or real estate deals. She was left alone with her parents and the others who still suffered the residual effects of the curse. The castle became more and more isolated, as if the briars had grown up again to surround the walls and those inside sleepwalked from room to room.

JULY

Temperature in the upper seventies, a bit of a breeze. Great cumulus clouds pass slowly through the summer sky like parade floats. And the slender grasses gather round you, pressing forward, with exaggerated deference, whispering, eager to catch a glimpse. It's your party after all. And it couldn't be more perfect. Yet there's a nagging thought: you don't really deserve all this attention, and that come October, there will be a price to pay.

I SAW MAMA KISSING SANTA CLAUS

What neither junior nor his father knows is that she sees him every time he phones. The off-season, mostly. So it isn't true that Santa only comes once a year. She does her hair, her makeup, and puts on the little black dress he likes so much, and her heels. She goes to meet him in some little out-of-the-way joint downtown. It's difficult for a high-profile guy like Santa to be discreet. What does she see in him anyway? Overweight and god knows how old, red-faced, slack-jawed and snoring now in room 308 of the Seafarer's Hotel? Well, it's true, he can be fun, his humor and generosity are legendary. But she sees this can't last. Perhaps though, despite her slight feeling of disappointment and the obvious impossibility of the whole affair, she still holds out some faint hope. A belief in something wondrous about to happen, that somehow this year will be better than last.

A SENSE OF DIRECTION

I hope no one reads anything I've written with the expectation of finding any meaning or direction. I have no sense of direction whatsoever. Yet occasionally, as I walk along in my private fog, someone will stop—and probably saying to himself, "Here's a guy who's obviously been around here for a hundred years"— ask how to get from wherever we are, to say—the Mariner Mall or the Saratoga. So I oblige this person with detailed instructions accompanied by elaborate gestures, pointing, and maps drawn in the air. We part mutually gratified, each feeling a sense of accomplishment. Later, I realize that my account had fatal flaws, and I imagine the lost soul saying, "What an idiot!" or "What a liar." Nevertheless, there are a lot of books out there, and a few of them actually contain accurate information. But these books all have the same limitation, they were written for the living. One is only alive for a short while and dead for a very long time. Yet, as far as I know, no one has written anything that's of any use to the dead.

III

RETIREMENT

I've been thinking of retiring, of selling the poetry business and enjoying my twilight years. It's a prose poem business, so it's a niche market. Still, after thirty some years, I must have assets worth well in excess of $300. Perhaps the new owner of the business will want to diversify, go into novels or plays, or perhaps merge into a school or a movement. It won't matter to me once I've retired. Maybe I'll do a little traveling, winter in the Southwest. Take up golf. Spend more time with the family. Maybe I'll just walk around and look at things with absolutely no compulsion to say anything at all about them.

AUTUMN LEAVES

"And you call yourself a poet!" she said walking toward me. It was a woman I recognized, though I couldn't remember her name. "Here you are on the most beautiful day of autumn... You should be writing a poem." "It's a difficult subject to write about, the fall," I said. "Nevertheless," she said, "I saw you drinking in the day, the pristine blue sky, the warm sunshine, the brilliant leaves of the maples and birches rustled slightly by the cool west wind which is the harbinger of winter. I saw how you watched that maple leaf fall. I saw how you picked it up and noted the flame color, touched here and there with bits of gold and green and tiny black spots. I know that you saw in that falling leaf all the glory and pathos, the joy and heartache of life on earth and yet you never touched pen to paper. "Actually," I said, "most of what I write is simply made up, not real at all." "So . . . ?" she said.

HALDEMAN & ERLICHMAN

Very few people remember Haldeman & Erlichman, and even fewer know which is which. Which goes to show that even infamy is fleeting. "Haldeman & Erlichman . . ." people say, "Haldeman & Erlichman. One of them is dead. I'm sure of that. Maybe both of them are dead." Haldeman & Erlichman, one the lesser known of those comedy teams that include Burns and Allen, Abbott and Costello, Martin and Lewis, Hamilton and Burr. Haldeman & Erlichman still play county fairs and Republican fundraisers in places like Keokuk or Kokomo. They appear at Henry Kissinger's annual birthday party. They sing, they do magic tricks. "Hi! I'm Haldeman!" "I'm Erlichman! One of us has a crew cut. Can you guess which one?"

MIDDLE AGES

Now we have arrived at our middle ages, our own private Middle Ages. It is a time of poverty and ignorance, the king's knights trampling the fields, the peasant's hovel on fire, the pigs loose in the cabbage patch. And from behind the monastery walls, comes the sound of mournful singing. It is an age of faith, I suppose. . . . So, what comes next? It seems to me that we must be going backwards. We long ago passed the Age of Enlightenment. It must be the Dark Ages. Already ravens have gathered in the oak tree and the long ships have hoisted their black sails to set forth on stormy seas that are the color of your eyes.

AWAKENING

When I open my eyes it appears that I'm still here, same hands, same feet, same room, you still here beside me as you have been, thankfully, for years, and the early light coming in the window as it always has. But appearances, as we know, can be deceiving. I'm putting on my white tie, baby, put your blue dress on! Let's go out there and see how many people we can fool.

APPLE DOLLS

To look at their faces you'd think they remembered child-
hoods of summer, long hours at the old swimmin' hole,
hayrides, blueberry pie, the county fair, kisses stolen under a
sky full of stars. You'd think those wrinkles came from many
years working the fields, the women cooking, washing clothes,
raising a dozen kids. But, as they were born old, in their clean
overalls and gingham dresses, they are perfect rubes, literally
born yesterday. They don't even remember last week's bingo
game or Tuesday's "Meals on Wheels" lunch, and indeed, that
may be the reason for all this rosy-cheeked merriment.

THE ASH GROVE

The black ash is the last tree to grow leaves in the spring and the first to lose them in the fall. Broken limbs, ragged bark all patchy with lichen, they scrape by in the swamp where not much else will grow. Most of the year it's difficult to say if they are dead or alive. And today with a low overcast sky and a cold wind blowing they look even more forlorn. So, I have a lot of sympathy for the black ash tree.

I walk out here to clear my head, which really isn't necessary because there really isn't much going on in there. Most of what I'm told goes in one ear and out the other. I stop and listen. Nothing but wind in the trees. Oh, but what if I forget everything? What if I forget how to tie my shoelaces or blow my nose? And the forest all around heaves a great sigh.

DINER

The time has come to say goodbye, our plates empty except for our greasy napkins. Comrades, you on my left, balding, middle-aged guy with a ponytail, and you, Lefty, there on my right, though we barely spoke I feel our kinship. You were steadfast in passing the ketchup, the salt and pepper, no man could ask for better companions. Lunch is over, the cheeseburgers and fries, the Denver sandwich, the counter nearly empty. Now we must go our separate ways. Not a fond embrace, but perhaps a hearty handshake. No? Well then, farewell. It is unlikely I'll pass this way again. Unlikely we will all meet again on this earth, to sit together beneath the neon and fluorescent calmly sipping our coffee, like the sages sipping their tea underneath the willow, sitting quietly, saying nothing.

FICTIONAL CHARACTER

They called me into an office, told me how much they liked my work, appreciated my loyalty, etc. In the end, they handed me a pistol, showed me how to shoot it and told me that I had to get rid of Edgar because Edgar was a danger to the organization, perhaps even a threat to national security. What organization? I thought this was an advertising agency. The problem is that I have a lousy author, a ham-handed hack. He goes for action and suspense: cheap tricks. Besides that, I rather like Edgar. He is described as "handsome, athletic, good natured, not given to introspection." Then there's Holly, beautiful Holly. We've just started going out together, things are going well between us, and it could lead to a "deeper relationship." Why would I want to ruin that? Any author will tell you that, finally, he has no control over his characters. Once created, they have a will of their own and go their own way. So, I told them I would have to think about it. I took the pistol and locked it in my desk drawer. I wondered if I should call the police. The thing I had not anticipated was what happened when I introduced Edgar to Holly.

OLD COUPLE

They walk hand-in-hand through the park. They must be well into their eighties and probably neither remembers exactly how they got together in the first place. It was so long ago. They are almost the same height and nearly the same shape in their matching sweaters and walking shorts. They walk very slowly. It looks as though either, or both, could fall over any minute. They hold hands the way they did when they first met, for hours, until their palms became sweaty. Both afraid that if they loosened the grip, the moment would be lost, that their happiness would somehow vanish. Now they hold hands to steady one another in a world that seems so terribly changed. This is a kind of tug-of-war as well. Which will tire first, lose interest, and let go?

HITCHHIKER

I pick up thistles and burdock, seeds of all sorts, on my pants legs as I walk the fields and ditches. Somewhere, way down the road, some will fall on fertile ground and begin the haphazard garden all over again. I pick up pebbles in my shoe treads and when they fall out they spawn streambeds, glacial eskers, mountain ranges. One day there will be a huge boulder right where your house is now, but it will take awhile.

KNIFE ISLAND

From Stoney Point it appears as a green, rounded shape in Superior's waters, perhaps safe haven, the Promised Land, like the Lake Isle of Innesfree rising from the mist. Up close it's just a pile of rocks with a few stunted trees, a place beaten by water and wind, a squalor of seagulls. The whole place is covered with gulls, gull shit, feathers and broken eggs, gulls in the air, gulls on the water, gulls on the ground. It's a noisy place, threat and intimidation, outrage, and indignation, the constant squabbling over territory. Their cry, "Justice!" "You are in my space!" Seagulls, like humans, not comfortable alone, not happy together. This is life with all its horrible enthusiasm, better seen from a distance.

STEADY OR SLOWLY FALLING

Around this time every year, the gloom swallows up someone unexpectedly, at random, it seems. We try to find reasons: *He was depressed. He ate too much sugar.* It seems hopeless, trying to figure things out. And yet, someone figured out the lever and the inclined plane. Someone invented glue and learned which mushrooms were good to eat. Thank god it wasn't all left to you, you can't even boil water. But there's no use whining that your parents didn't leave you proper instructions or adequate tools, you simply have to make do. A stick to dig roots and grubs for the soup, and you have learned, by now, that it takes only a light tap with the same stick to put the baby down for his nap. Now, with the snow falling outside, the soup bubbling in the pot, the baby sleeping soundly in his crib, there's time for a moment of reflection. . . . Then the phone rings, and the baby starts crying just as the pot on the stove boils over, and, between one thing and another, your feet get tangled in the phone line. Which is a length of string tied to a couple of tin cans.

PARK

You could think of it as a small park. Well, not exactly a park, a little space between two busy streets, a city beautification project, an afterthought of city planners, all nicely bricked, with a park bench and an old maple tree that predates any planning, nothing else. It's a space nobody uses, really. Nobody sits on the bench. The drunks throw empty wine bottles here, now and then. And occasionally a bird, a crow or a sparrow, lands on a bare branch of the tree, on its way elsewhere. You could think of the leaves that have fallen as all of your dreams and hopes that have fallen and blown away, now that it is November. But there is no park really, and no bare branch where a bird could land. There is only this empty space that you cherish and protect, where once your heart was.

TIME MARCHES ON

How quickly the days are passing, Crazy Days, Wrong Days in Wright, Rutabaga Days, Duck Days, Red Flannel Days. Gone the Black Fly Festival, the Eelpout Festival, Finn Fest, the Carnivore's Ball, the Five-Mile-Long Rummage Sale; all have passed. What has passed is forever lost. Modern Dance on the Bridge Abutment, The Hardanger Fiddle Association of America Meeting, the Polka Mass, "O, lost and by the wind grieved . . . " The Inline Skate Marathon, the Jet Ski Grand Prix . . . What is past is as though it never was. The Battle of the Bands, the Polar Bear Plunge, the Monster Truck Challenge, the Poetry Slam. . .

IV

SUBLIMATION

In scientific terms, sublimation is the direct conversion, under certain pressure and temperature conditions, of a solid into a gas, bypassing the liquid state. That's why that patch of ice on the sidewalk gets a little smaller every day even though the temperature never gets above zero. Something similar happens whenever I deposit a check into my bank account. The funds never reach a liquid state. It's the same when, thirty years later, you visit the house you lived in as a child. It's much smaller than you remember. People are older and smaller. Everyone notices when something dramatic happens, a car crash, a tree falling over. They whine about the drive-in movie theater closing down. Yet the subtle process of the sublime goes on continually, without much notice. Whatever was, continues to be, in the form of molecules or atoms or something, no more available now than it was back then.

THE LONG WINTER

The winter here is so long that one needs to find an outdoor activity to pass the time. Some people ski or snowboard. There's snowmobiling, ice skating, hockey. . . I prefer ice fishing. Standing around in the cold wind all day, pulling ice fish from a hole in the ice. Ice fish have to be eaten raw, like sushi. If you cook an ice fish you wind up with nothing but a skillet full of water. Gnash one down or swallow it whole, there is nothing like the flavor, full of the glittering, bitter cold of a January day. Your teeth crack, your tongue goes numb, your lips turn blue and your eyes roll back in your head. "God!" you say, "God that was good! Let me have just one more."

AN ILL WIND

Today there's a cold northeast wind blowing, piling up ice all along the water's edge. The Point is deserted, no one for five miles down the beach. Just the way I like it. The sand is frozen mostly, so the walking is easy as I pick my way through the wrack and drift. Today I don't even leave footprints. Wind, sand, sun and water. A simplicity that defies comprehension. The barest essentials for the imagination's work. This shore has been pretty much the same for ten thousand years. Countless others have been here before me, musing and pondering, as they walked down the beach and disappeared forever. So here's what I'm thinking: wouldn't it be great if one of them dropped a big roll of hundred dollar bills and I found it?

I MUST SAY

Now that we have come so far together, so much water gone under the bridge, and now that the shadows lengthen around us, I feel that I must say some things that are difficult for me to say. . . . This is a world of plague bearing prairie dogs and freshly fried flesh. Where is the fish sauce shop, and when did the Irish wristwatch shop shut? Are our oars oak? Are the sheep asleep in the shed? I cannot give you specific statistics, but surely the sun will shine soon. Surely the sun will shine on the stop signs and on the twin-screw steel cruisers.

I have lain awake nights thinking of how to say this. I can only hope that what these words lack in meaning will be somehow compensated for by your understanding of my need to say them, and by your knowing that these words are meant for you. Though who you are in this context is never made clear, and it is quite possible that you, yourself, do not know.

THE BLACK JOURNAL

In the black journal there are a number of entries about the weather and the slant of the winter light. There is an observation of how sea smoke rises from the cooling body of water, along with some unintelligible scribbling about form and substance. On page 21 there are a few ideas for financial reorganization. Then on page 23 some notes about ice fishing. After that there are many, many blank pages.

DARK DAYS

Overcast skies, the threat of snow, the day is a lingering twilight that makes these big white pines seem even more ominous. At any moment one of these old trees could fall, killing me instantly. Here's what the investigating officer told the newspapers: "It was an act of God, pure and simple. Some people don't believe in God's existence but something like this just goes to prove it." Which causes me to wonder, was it predestined or just a moment of extreme annoyance? The forest gives rise to such gloomy speculations. We stand around, no real answers, not much to say, and nothing to do until another wind comes along, sending us into a fury of pointless activity.

LOST

It's remarkable, the honesty people exhibit in regard to lost mittens, particularly, a single mitten, and really that is all you ever see. The finder picks up the mitten and places it in a prominent place, on a tree branch or a window ledge, where it can be easily spotted by the searcher. Days go by, but the owner of the mitten does not return. A mitten lost is gone forever, separated from its mate for eternity. It's always that way it seems. One mitten, one shoe on the freeway, one nearly new sock alone in the drawer, having never really gotten to know its missing partner. But here at Lover's Overlook, there's a *pair* of panties, a splash of bright red in the weeds. One imagines mayhem or, possibly, wild celebration. But no one expects the owner to retrieve the lost item.

GOINGS ON AROUND THE HOUSE

There's a spider crawling across the crown molding and I don't like the looks of him. I know you can learn by watching spiders. I know about Robert the Bruce and Whitman's noiseless, patient spider. But maybe Whitman's hearing wasn't all that good, maybe that spider was going about his work whistling, a kind of annoying, tuneless whistle. Whitman said he could go and live with the animals, and people do. Generally, though, we tend to be rather choosy about which animals. People often want a certain breed of dog or cat, nothing else will do. Of course, there are people who live with rats and snakes, and god knows what else. I don't care. There is a spider on my ceiling and I don't like him.

OLD FRIENDS

There's a game we play, not a game exactly, a sort of call and response. It's one of the pleasures of living for a long time in a fairly small place. "You know, they lived over by Plett's Grocery." "Where that bank is now?" "That's right." "Plett's, I'd almost forgotten. Do you remember where Ward's was?" "Didn't they tear it down to build the Holiday Mall?" "Yes." "I remember. The Holiday Mall." It works for people, too. "Remember the guy who came to all the art exhibit openings, the guy with the hat?" "Yeah, he came for the free food and drinks?" "Right." "And there was the guy with the pipe and the tweed jacket who always said hello to everyone because he wasn't sure who he actually knew." "Oh, yes!" It's like the words to an old song, *la, la, la,* some of which you remember. And after I have gone someone will say, "Oh *him.* I thought he was still around. I used to see him everywhere, only, all this time, I thought he was someone else."

THE STATE OF THE ECONOMY

There might be some change on top of the dresser at the back, and we should check the washer and the dryer. Check under the floor mats of the car. The couch cushions. I have some books and CDs I could sell, and there are a couple of big bags of aluminum cans in the basement, only trouble is that there isn't enough gas in the car to get around the block. I'm expecting a check sometime next week, which, if we are careful, will get us through to payday. In the meantime with your one-dollar rebate check and a few coins we have enough to walk to the store and buy a quart of milk and a newspaper. On second thought, forget the newspaper.

REMEMBER

I'm trying to take up less space. I'm trying to remember to pick up after myself, to remember to take off my muddy boots before I come into the house. It's difficult. Partly because one branch of my family can trace their lineage directly back to an extinct species of water buffalo. I have to learn to talk quietly. To eat slowly, keeping my mouth closed. To wash and dry my little bowl and spoon and put them away. Turn off the lights, close the door softly. Descend the stairs carefully, avoiding the step that creaks, so as not to wake the dead who are sleeping shoulder to shoulder. Those so long dead that their names and dates have eroded from their tombstones. The dead who can turn over in their narrow graves without ever touching the body next to them.

OF AN AGE

I'm getting to an age when, if I suddenly dropped dead, most people would not be overly surprised. And, no doubt, there are some who would welcome the news. I'm not particularly looking forward to it—death and whatever comes after. Which is not much by the look of it, decomposition and discorporation, when all the microorganisms that make up this conglomerate go their separate ways, thus ending one instance of corporate greed and mismanagement. But possibly some will linger, talk of an employee buyout, some wearing buttons that say "Solidarity Forever." Most likely, there will be a few farewell parties with drinks and reminiscing, balloons, a joke sign saying, "Will the last to leave please turn out the lights?"

SOME THINGS TO THINK ABOUT

How cold is it? Will you need to wear your longjohns or will the heavy wool pants over your blue jeans be enough? Which socks? Which boots? Which jacket? Scarf? Do you need the choppers with wool liners or just gloves? How fast will you be moving? If you are skiing or, God forbid, going to the mall, will you be too warm? Which direction is the wind from? Is it better to walk into the wind on your way out and have it at your back on the return, or vise-versa? Do you have a choice? Will the car start? Do you have blankets, fire extinguisher, flares, window scraper, extra gasoline, gas-line antifreeze, starting fluid, lock deicer, windshield washer fluid, a shovel, fresh water, flashlight, matches, candy bars? Do you have enough Kleenex? Ask yourself what you have forgotten. Do not ask yourself why or how. Remember to take your car keys out of your pocket before you put on your gloves.

THE CHAIR

The chair has four legs but is a whole lot slower moving than, for instance, the ostrich, which has only two. Sometimes the chair does not move for weeks, even months at a time. Though, it could be argued that the chair is every bit as intelligent as the ostrich, whose brain is smaller than its eye. And the chair is far less dangerous and unpredictable than the ostrich. The chair is more thoroughly domesticated. But it isn't a lazy boy. Don't slouch, don't lean back too far or the chair will throw you, for sure. The chair invites you to relax but to remain upright and attentive. The chair invites you to come to the table, sit down and eat your big bowl of ostrich stew.

WAYFARING STRANGER

There are places in the world that, because of time and money or inclination, I am never going to visit: Iquitos, for instance, or Archangel, the Ross Ice Shelf, Baltimore. There are places in the woods just outside town where I will probably never go. There may be a square foot or two of swampland out there where no human being has ever stepped, or at least, not for a long time. There is an outside chance I might wind up there one day. There are parts of my own back yard where I hardly ever go, especially in winter when the ground is covered with snow. And then, even when spring beckons, I often decline the invitation. Inside any house there are remote and seldom visited corners. Suppose you found yourself behind a closet door, or in the dusty attic, in the damp recesses of the basement, in the company of spiders and sow bugs. You might come to yourself slightly exhilarated, but uneasy, a bit heartsick so far away from home.

THE SNOWMAN MONOLOGUES

I don't have the top hat like my ancestors . . . well, my prede-
cessors, had. I've got one of these little snap-brim caps like
English motorists and golfers wear and a very nice scarf. Quite
bon vivant, I think. I've had to give up the pipe and I never drink.
Still, I've got a big smile for everyone. I'm a traditionalist. I like
the old songs, "White Christmas," "Ain't Misbehavin'," "Don't
Get Around Much Anymore," songs like that. But I try to stay
up to date, try to be aware of what's happening. I'm very
concerned about global warming, for instance, but it's difficult
in my field to get any real information. And what can I do?
Not that I'm complaining. I like it here; I feel at home, very
much a part of my environment. It does get lonely at times
though, there are so very few women in these parts and I'm
not the best looking guy around, with my strange build and
very odd nose. Sometimes I think they put my nose in the
wrong place. Still, I have always hoped that someone would
come along, someone who would melt in my arms. A woman
with whom I could become one. You wouldn't guess it to look
at me, but I'm a romantic. But it's getting rather late in the
season for me. So, I'm inclined just to drift. . . . I don't have
any problems getting through the night; it's the days that are
so long and difficult now that spring is coming. Oh, spring is
beautiful with the new buds on the trees and the bright
sunshine, but it's such a melancholy season. It causes one to
reflect. . . . Oh, but here I go, running off at the mouth again.

WEDNESDAY

Wednesday is named after Odin (Wotan) the chief of the Norse gods. Odin was in tough shape. He had an extremely difficult and painful education. He had one eye. He was anorexic and had a drinking problem. He had an eight-legged horse, a couple of wolves and two ravens, Thought and Memory, that flew all over the world but, presumably, returned to him on occasion.

The French word for Wednesday is *mercredi*, after the Roman god Mercury, a naked guy with wings on his heels, who went around delivering messages and flowers. He moved very quickly.

It is a windy, winter Wednesday as I write. Today is washday, there's a pot of beans boiling on the kitchen stove, steam condensing on the cold windowpanes. And today is the birthday of George Washington, the father of our country. "Wednesday's child is full of woe." So the nursery rhyme goes, but George Washington did all right, despite a couple of hard winters. Still, he was no barrel of laughs, either.

Wednesday is known as "hump day," halfway through the workweek, a hill from which you can view the road you are traveling, to where it vanishes in the haze at either horizon. On one side of the road trees in shadow, on the other trees in sun, and sometimes between the tall trunks, a glimpse of clear blue sky.

EXPANDING UNIVERSE

Not just the galaxies, everything is moving farther apart. That's why when I reached out for that glass, it fell and shattered after a long, long fall to the floor. That is why I missed the first step going upstairs. And I so rarely see my friends anymore, seldom see them rise above the horizon: a distant glimmer in the darkening firmament. And you and I, have we grown apart as well? I smile and wink, wave to you there on the far side of the bed.

UP IN THE MORNING

"I don't belong here," I tell myself over and over. "I was never good at swimming and I have no sense of direction." Once again I'm lost and can't find the opening. I manage to breathe by sticking my nose into the little pockets of air just beneath the ice, gasping. . . Then suddenly, by some miracle, over there, not fifty feet away, the light shining down from the other world. I haul my ass out onto the ice sheet. At last. I can warm my blubber in the sunshine, have a cup of coffee, some orange juice, maybe have one or two of those little almond cookies, read a bit of the newspaper, find out what's happening in New York and Los Angeles, perhaps even smoke a cigar before I'm noticed.

WRONG TURN

Because you missed your turn two miles back you have decided to turn on the wrong road, just because you are too lazy to turn around. You have decided to turn here just because of some vague notion. You have decided to turn here just because you aren't smart enough not to. You have decided to turn here . . . just because. Listen, help is available. There are people who have experience with this kind of thing, people who have been through this. There are hotlines. There are brochures. There are programs, support groups. There is financial aid. Listen. The angels gather around you like gnats, strumming their guitars, singing songs of salvation, singing songs of freedom and diversity. But you aren't listening. Here you are on the *genuine* road less traveled. The road never snowplowed. Nothing to do but follow the ruts. Here the snow is too deep to turn around. You are going to have to follow this road to whatever nowhere it leads.

Louis Jenkins lives in Duluth, Minnesota. His poems have been published in a number of literary magazines and anthologies. His books of poetry include *An Almost Human Gesture* (Eighties Press and Ally Press, 1987), *All Tangled Up With the Living* (Nineties Press, 1991), *Nice Fish: New and Selected Prose Poems* (Holy Cow! Press, 1995), *Just Above Water* (Holy Cow! Press, 1997) and *The Winter Road* (Holy Cow! Press, 2000). Some of his prose poems were published in *The Best American Poetry, 1999* (Scribner, 1999) and in *Great American Prose Poems* (Scribner, 2003).